BE AN ACTIVE
CITIZEN
IN YOUR
COMMUNITY

Helen Mason

🌳 **Crabtree Publishing Company**
www.crabtreebooks.com

CITIZENSHIP IN ACTION

Author: Helen Mason

Series research and development: Reagan Miller

Editors: Petrice Custance and Reagan Miller

Proofreader: Janine Deschenes

Design and photo research: Margaret Amy Salter

Prepress technician: Margaret Amy Salter

Print and production coordinator: Katherine Berti

Photographs

iStockphoto: cover
Shutterstock.com: Joseph Sohm: page 8; littleny: page 9;
    Anita van den Broek: page 19

All other images from Shutterstock

Library and Archives Canada Cataloguing in Publication

Mason, Helen, 1950-, author
    Be an active citizen in your community / Helen Mason.

(Citizenship in action)
Includes index.
Issued in print and electronic formats.
ISBN 978-0-7787-2601-2 (hardback).--
ISBN 978-0-7787-2607-4 (paperback).--
ISBN 978-1-4271-1778-6 (html)

    1. Social participation--Juvenile literature. 2. Community life--Juvenile
literature. 3. Political participation--Juvenile literature.I. Title.

HM771.M38 2016   j302'.14   C2016-904149-2
                                          C2016-904150-6

Library of Congress Cataloging-in-Publication Data

CIP available at the Library of Congress

Crabtree Publishing Company

www.crabtreebooks.com   1-800-387-7650

Printed in Canada/082016/TL20160715

Published in Canada
Crabtree Publishing
616 Welland Ave.
St. Catharines, Ontario
L2M 5V6

Published in the United States
Crabtree Publishing
PMB 59051
350 Fifth Avenue, 59th Floor
New York, New York 10118

Published in the United Kingdom
Crabtree Publishing
Maritime House
Basin Road North, Hove
BN41 1WR

Published in Australia
Crabtree Publishing
3 Charles Street
Coburg North
VIC 3058

What is in this book?

What is a community?

A **community** is a place where people live, work, and play. They live in houses and apartment buildings.

People in a community depend on each other. Farmers grow food. Store owners buy food from farmers and then sell it. Police officers keep the farms and stores safe. Electrical companies make sure that everyone has electricity. Everyone works together!

People also have fun in communities.
There are parks to explore. There are playgrounds
to enjoy. Some communities have swimming pools.
Others have arenas.

Many communities have museums and libraries. These are places to learn new things.

What is a citizen?

The people who live in a community are its **citizens**.

Citizens can be old or young.

Both grandparents and babies are citizens.

You are a citizen too!

Citizens have **rights**. A right is something you are allowed to have or do. You have the right to ride your bike.

Citizens also have a **responsibility** to make their community a great place for everyone. A responsibility is something you should take care of or do. You have a responsibility to obey your community's **rules**. Rules keep people safe.

You follow the rules when you wear a helmet while riding your bike.

What is an active citizen?

Active citizens help make their communities great places to live.

Some active citizens work with people who are new to the community. They welcome new people and help them learn about the community.

Other active citizens work to keep rivers and lakes clean. They help fish and other animals stay healthy. They make sure the water is safe to drink.

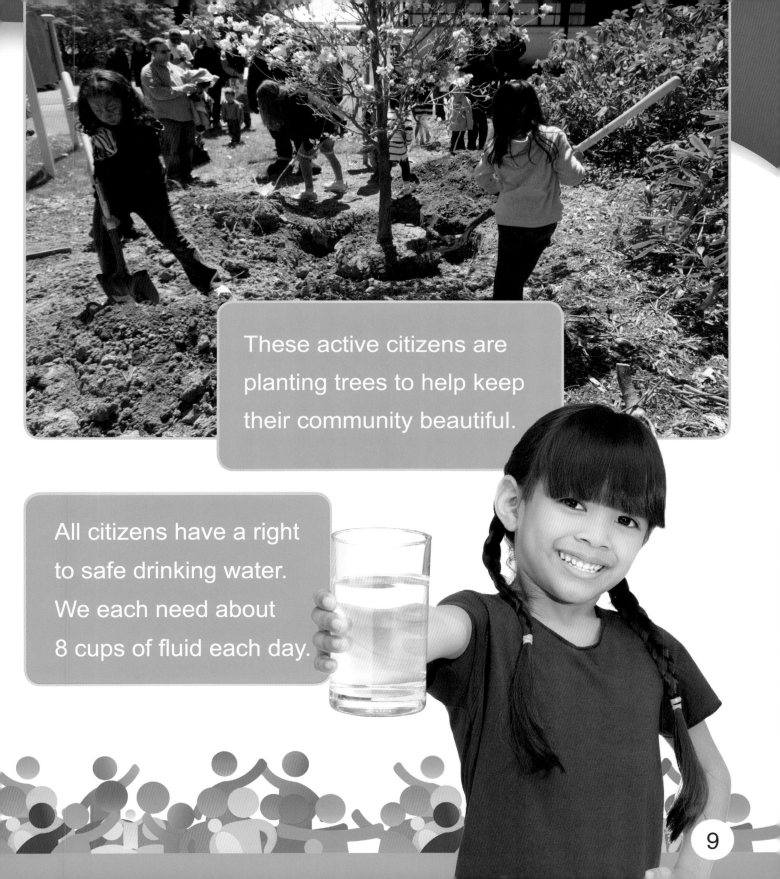

These active citizens are planting trees to help keep their community beautiful.

All citizens have a right to safe drinking water. We each need about 8 cups of fluid each day.

What do active citizens do?

Every community has written and unwritten rules. Active citizens follow both types of rules.

Written rules are called **laws**. Laws are rules made by the **government** and **enforced** by police officers. Laws are made to keep everyone safe, such as how fast someone can drive a car.

Unwritten rules are rules everyone knows are the best way to behave with each other, such as being polite to your neighbor.

All active citizens follow three important unwritten rules:

 Show **respect**

 Play fair

 Help Others

These active citizens pick up garbage. What unwritten rules are they following?

Showing respect

Respect means you follow rules and laws to show you care about the rights of others.

People show respect in many ways.

- ☑ They say please and thank you.
- ☑ They listen to others.
- ☑ They compliment others.
- ☑ They offer help when people need it.

Communities have many different kinds of people. Some people come from different places. They may dress differently or eat different foods. Active citizens know it is good to be different. Active citizens show respect to everyone.

What do you think?

You are at a community pool. How can you show respect for others? Are any images on this page an example of not showing respect for others?

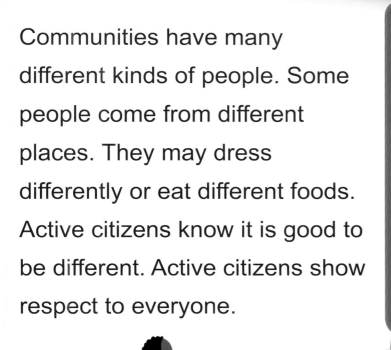

What is Earth Day?

Earth Day is on
April 22 each year. It is a time
when people show respect for the
environment. People in many
communities plan special
projects for Earth Day.

Some groups plant trees.

Some groups pick up garbage.

Families also celebrate Earth Day. Many families plan a project that helps Earth.

Some walk or ride a bicycle to school or work, instead of driving a car.

Others turn off the water while they brush their teeth.

What do you think?

Your family would like to do something to help the environment. They are discussing ideas. What suggestions can you make?

Playing fair

Do you play games and sports? Playing fair means you have a responsibility to learn the rules and follow them.

When people play fair:

 They share

 Everyone gets a turn

 No one is left out

Each game and sport has its own rules. The rules tell us how to play. They explain what each player can and cannot do. Rules say when the game ends.

When you play fair, everyone has a chance to win. When you follow the rules of a game or sport, it is fun for everyone. Imagine playing soccer but only some of the players were allowed to kick the ball. That would not be fair or fun!

Helping others

Communities are made up of families, friends, and neighbors. It feels good to help these people.

Helping starts at home. Active citizens do jobs around the house. They help with housework. They might also take care of the recycling.

Sometimes you can help in big ways. You can have a bottle drive. You can use the money to help build a safe playground.

Sometimes you can help in small ways. You can offer to rake leaves for a neighbor.

Helping others is how active citizens keep their community strong.

These kids are raising money for **charity**. Their donations help others.

Growing together

Community gardens are shared gardens. They are places where active citizens work together to make their community more beautiful. Active citizens can also share the fruits and vegetables they grow with their neighbors. Community gardens are great for the environment. Community gardens are great for everyone!

Children and adults dig the soil. They plant the seeds. They care for the plants. They pick and eat the fruits and vegetables. Yum!

What do you think?

There is a community garden near you. You would like to help. Your friend says that there's nothing you can do. Do you agree? What might you say and do to show what you think?

Learning more

Books

Chantler, Kaitlin, Delaina Arnold, and Glenda Clayton. *Kids in the Biosphere Activity Booklet.* Georgian Bay Biosphere Reserve, 2016.

Dalrymple, Lisa. *Be the Change in the World*. Crabtree Publishing Company, 2015.

Kopp, Megan. *Be the Change in your Community.* Crabtree Publishing Company, 2015.

Nielsen, Shelly. *Playing Fair.* Abdo & Daughters Publishing, 1991.

Web Sites

Learn about neighbors who help each other:
www.usd489.com/technology/textbooks/Grade_3_Book_2/Castle.htm

Find out why clean air is important and how you can help keep it that way:
www3.epa.gov/airnow/picturebook/cocos-orange-day-web.pdf

Get a coloring book about Earth-friendly ways to travel here:
www3.epa.gov/otaq/kids/420k03001.pdf

Words to Know

charity (CHAIR-it-ee) noun A group of people who collect money and other things for those who need them

citizens (SIT-i-senz) noun People who belong to a community

community (CU-mu-ni-tee) noun A place where people live, work, and play

enforce (en-FAWRS) verb To make sure a rule or law is followed

environment (en-VYE-ruhn-mhnt) noun The natural surroundings of living things

government [GUHV-ern-muhnt] noun A group of people that run a country, province, state, or community

laws (LAWZ) noun Rules made by government that people must follow

respect (re-SPECKED) noun To follow rules and laws to show you value the rights of others

responsibility (re-SPONS-i-bill-i-tee) noun Something you should take care of or do

right (RITE) noun Something you are allowed to have or do

rule (rool) noun The correct way to behave

A noun is a person, place, or thing.

A verb is an action word that tells you what someone or something does.

23

Index

About the author

Helen Mason currently volunteers at a drop-in center for teens. When she was in grades 2 and 3, her grandmother had a plot in a community garden. Helen carried tools, helped to weed and pick, and enjoyed eating carrots fresh from the earth. This is her 31st book.